BELIEFS AND CULTURES

Sikh

Catherine Chambers

Children's Press
A Division of Grolier Publishing
New York   Danbury, Connecticut   London
Hong Kong   Sydney

Library of Congress Cataloging-in-Publication
Data

Chambers, Catherine.
    Sikh / by Catherine Chambers.
        p. cm. — (Beliefs and Cultures)
    ISBN 0-516-08079-2
    1. Sikhism—Juvenile literature. I. Title. II
Series.
    BL2018.C53 1995   94-47348
    294.6—dc20   CIP AC

1996 Childrens Press® Edition
©1995 Watts Books
Printed in Great Britain
Published simultaneously in Canada

1 2 3 4 5 6 7 8 9 0 R 05 04 03 02 01 00 99 98
97 96

Series Editor: Sarah Ridley
Designer: Liz Black
Copy Editor: Nicola Barber
Illustrators: pg 27 Piers Harper, pg 7 Aziz Khan
Photographer (activities): Peter Millard

Photographs: Format 6, 20, 21b, 28, 29;
Hutchison Library 15b, 17b, 18t, 21t; Ann and
Bury Peerless cover (left), 4, 13; Frank Spooner
Pictures 7, 18b, 30b; Trip cover (right), 5, 8, 9,
10, 11, 14, 15t, 16, 17t, 22, 24, 25, 26, 30t.

Acknowledgements: with special thanks to
Kulvant Kaur Benning and her Panjabi class at
Edgewick Community Primary School, Coventry,
England.

CONTENTS

THE FIRST SIKHS

The Sikh religion is five hundred years old. It started with the teachings of Guru Nanak, the first Sikh Guru, who was born in 1469. Guru means "religious" or "wise teacher." Guru Nanak was born in a small village on the flat, green plain known as the Panjab. Today, this region extends across part of north-west India and into east Pakistan.

At the time of Guru Nanak's birth, most people in the Panjab followed one of two religions, Hinduism or Islam. Hinduism developed more than 3000 years ago in northern India. Islam, which is practiced by Muslims, began about 1400 years ago in Arabia. It was first brought to India in A.D. 711, and by the 12th century a huge Muslim Empire ruled over the Panjab and North India. Hindus and Muslims did not always get along well with each other. So Guru Nanak entered a world of conflict.

THE FIRST GURU

Guru Nanak was born into a Hindu family. He was a thoughtful person, deeply troubled by the divisions between Hindus and Muslims. Guru Nanak received messages from God, telling him to go out and teach people how to follow a simple faith.

Guru Nanak traveled far, preaching his message. Guru Nanak hoped that if people concentrated on living as God wanted them to, the differences between them would melt away. Those who followed Guru Nanak's teachings were called "Sikhs." In the Panjabi language, Sikh means "learner."

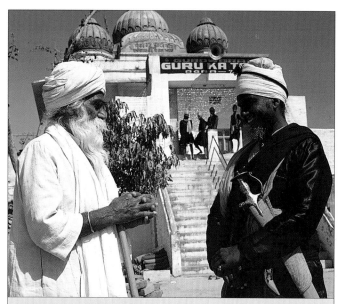

Two Sikhs in traditional dress chat outside a *gurdwara*, or Sikh temple, in Agra, a town outside the Panjab, India.

NEW WAYS OF THINKING

Over many years, Guru Nanak patiently told people how they could live more as God wished. He taught that people who were really trying to lead good lives should pray and meditate on God's name in a simple, humble way. They should work hard and with honesty, care for their families, and serve the community. They should not gather great wealth around them.

Lots of pictures of Guru Nanak can be seen in Sikh communities around the world.

SINGING GOD'S WORD

Guru Nanak made God's teachings into poems. Mardana, one of the Guru's Muslim friends, composed and played music for them. So the poems became hymns, which were remembered and passed on.

This fresco, or wall painting, shows the young Guru Nanak left in charge of some cattle.

Most Sikhs will recognize this right away! It is the Mul Mantra, written in Gurmukhi script (top three lines only).

Before he died, the Guru chose his most trusted friend, Bhai Lehna, to become the next Guru. *Bhai* means "brother" among Sikhs, and is a term showing great respect. Guru Nanak gave Lehna a new name, Angad, which means "my limb." Angad was Guru Nanak's closest friend and helper. The Guru also felt that Angad was a part of him, so the name suited him well. Soon after Angad had been chosen, Guru Nanak died. Guru Angad was now the new teacher.

THE GURU'S TRAVELS
Guru Nanak traveled around the Panjab, teaching his message.

Sometimes a small group of people gathered around him. At other times, huge crowds swarmed at his feet. Guru Nanak also made four great journeys. He is said to have traveled north into the mountains, and south to Sri Lanka. He went west to Makkah and east to Assam.

THE SIKH WORLD
Since then, Sikhs have also traveled taking the teachings of the Gurus with them. One group to leave India were soldiers. They joined the British Army after Britain took over the Panjab in 1849. When the army went overseas, some Sikh soldiers decided to stay in Great Britain.

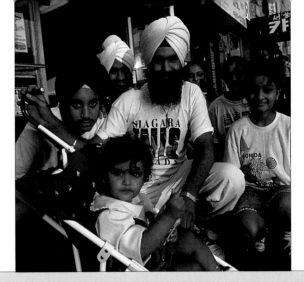

A Sikh family shows a happy mixture of traditional and Western culture in New York City.

For hundreds of thousands of Sikhs, the Panjab is now a foreign place. Sikh temples, called *gurdwaras*, have been built at the heart of Sikh communities in many countries. Some Sikhs keep traditional ways, while others have more Western lifestyles. Some speak fluent Panjabi, others speak different languages. But all are Sikhs and can trace their beliefs and culture back to the Panjab and the teachings of the first Guru.

Most Sikhs who have settled outside India, live in towns and cities. Many are now moving to the cities of Europe and the Middle East.

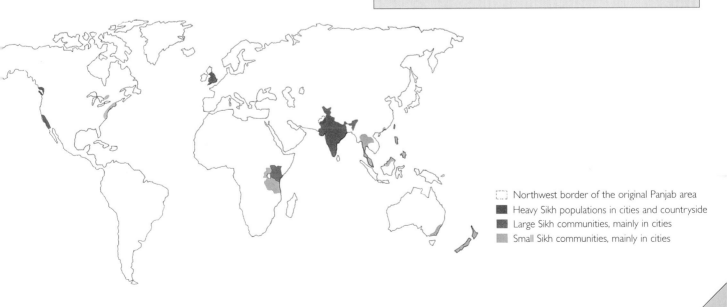

☐ Northwest border of the original Panjab area
■ Heavy Sikh populations in cities and countryside
■ Large Sikh communities, mainly in cities
■ Small Sikh communities, mainly in cities

ONLY TEN GURUS

Guru Nanak is surrounded by the other nine Gurus. You can see the youngest Guru, Guru Har Krishan, who died of smallpox in Delhi, India.

SPOTLIGHT

THE TEN GURUS	BIRTH	DEATH
Guru Nanak	1469	1539
Guru Angad	1504	1552
Guru Amar Das	1479	1574
Guru Ram Das	1534	1581
Guru Arjan	1563	1606
Guru Hargovind	1595	1644
Guru Har Rai	1630	1661
Guru Har Krishan	1656	1664
Guru Tegh Bahadur	1621	1675
Guru Govind Singh	1666	1708

Just before Guru Nanak died, he chose Guru Angad to take his place. Eight other Gurus followed, each Guru naming his successor. The Gurus were chosen for their belief in God, their humble ways, and their search for the truth. Each Guru is remembered today for giving Sikhism something special.

GURU ANGAD'S ALPHABET

Sikhs follow the teachings in the hymns composed by some of the Gurus. Today, the verses can be read, but when Guru Nanak was alive they were passed from one Sikh community to another by word of mouth.

Guru Angad, the second Guru, looked after Guru Nanak's hymns. It was not easy to remember them all, so he started to write them down. This was difficult, as there were several ways of writing the script. It is thought that Guru Angad developed the final version of the Gurmukhi alphabet, in which the hymns are still read (see page 6).

Langar is sometimes eaten in a dining room with table and chairs. At the Harimandir, the huge temple in Amritsar, India, langar is eaten outside.

EATING TOGETHER

Sharing a meal is an important Sikh tradition. In every gurdwara, there is a dining room where people can eat together. Here, everyone — Sikh or non-Sikh — is welcome. Like Guru Nanak, Guru Amar Das, the third Guru, felt that eating together was a symbol of harmony and equality. But, unlike Guru Nanak, as well as inviting people to sit and eat with him, he set up an open dining room, called a *langar*, where everyone was welcome. Anyone who wanted to see the Guru had to go to the langar room first and eat happily with anyone who was there. The meal itself was also called *langar*.

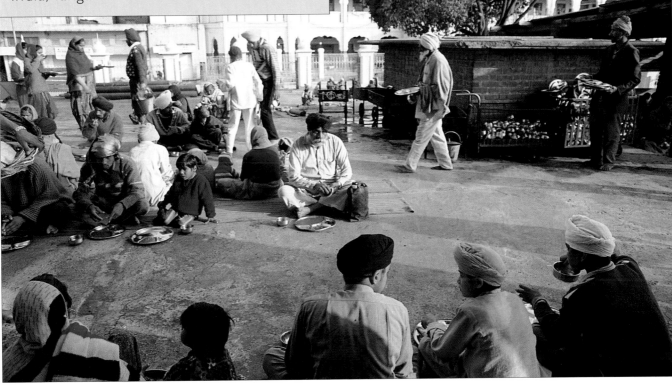

THE GURUS BUILD A CITY FOR SIKHS

Amritsar is a city in the Indian Panjab with a magnificent temple at its heart. It was built as a place where the Gurus' hymns could be stored safely. The city also became a center of learning and culture for the Sikh community. It is visited every year by thousands of Sikhs from all over the world.

Guru Amar Das, the third Guru, started creating the city by enlarging a sacred pool — "a pool of nectar"— which is the meaning of the name "Amritsar." It is said that the land used by the Guru had been given to his daughter by the Muslim ruler, Emperor Akbar. The emperor had great respect for Guru Amar Das.

The pool around the temple is really a huge tank. When it is cleaned out, thousands of people come to help.

Children enjoy taking a dip in the pool in the early morning.

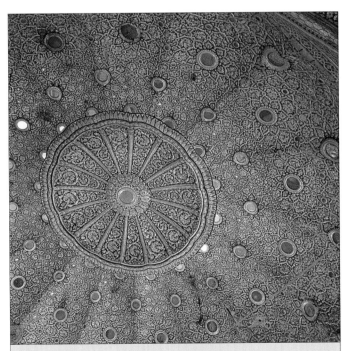

The dome of the Harimandir is lined with shining mirrors set in gold, a form of decoration used at the time.

The Guru chose his son-in-law as the fourth Guru. It was he, Guru Ram Das, who built the city of Amritsar next to the sacred pool. Guru Ram Das's son and successor, Guru Arjan, lined the pool with bricks and built a temple in it. The temple was called "Harimandir" — the temple of God. It has since been rebuilt several times but now looks more or less as it did nearly 400 years ago. Today, it is also known as the "Golden Temple." This is because the upper stories were covered with copper panels gilded with gold in the 19th century.

DECORATIONS IN THE HARIMANDIR

WHAT TO DO:

1 Make some papier mâché by tearing newspaper into small pieces and soaking them in water and flour, or paste, overnight.

2 Glue a sheet of foil smoothly over your piece of cardboard. Squeeze the water out of the papier mâché and mold it into shapes on the cardboard, leaving holes for the "mirrors." Let it dry overnight.

3 Paint the dry papier mâché a bright color and glue on sequins and bits of colored cellophane.

DEFENDING THE SIKH FAITH

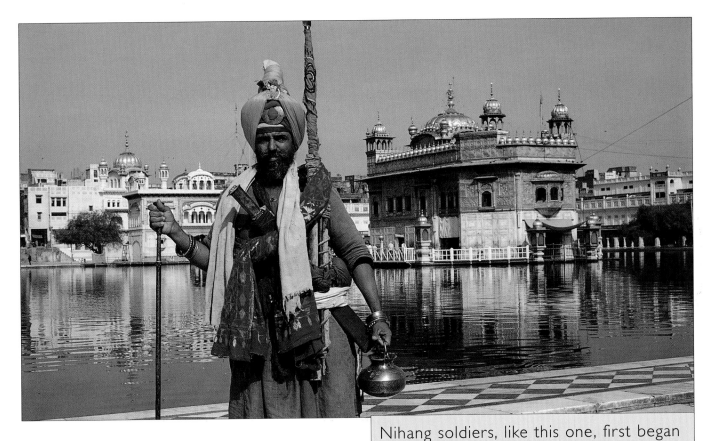

Nihang soldiers, like this one, first began as a fierce fighting force over 200 years ago.

GURU ARJAN'S IMPORTANT TASK

Guru Arjan built the Harimandir as a safe place to keep the Gurus' hymns, where no one could alter them. The Guru realized that it was best to collect the hymns together and bind them into a book. Copies could then be made for Sikhs who lived far away. So the Guru asked one of his companions, Bhai Gurdas, to gather all the Gurus' verses. They were to include the *bhagat bhani*, the hymns written by some Hindus and Muslims, whose teachings about God and life were similar to those of the Gurus. The great book was compiled in 1604. Guru Arjan called it *Adi Granth*, the "first book," meaning "the most important." It was placed in the Harimandir, in the hands of the first *granthi* — a person who looks after the book. Bhai Budha, an old and trusted friend of the Gurus, was given this honored task. Today, granthis, who can be men or women, still care for the book in their gurdwaras.

A NEED FOR STRENGTH...

Sikhs often felt that their way of life was threatened. Sometimes they had to defend themselves against the Muslim rulers of the Panjab. A crisis came when Guru Tegh Bahadur, the ninth Guru, was killed by the Muslim emperor of India, Aurangzeb. The Guru's son, Guru Govind Singh, finally felt forced to create a Sikh army. But the army was only supposed to fight if the Sikh community was attacked.

These four symbols, along with uncut hair, make up the five "Ks."

... AND A NEED FOR DISCIPLINE

Each Sikh community has a group of people who promise to live by very strict rules. These men and women are identified by five special things in their appearance. The group is known as the *Khalsa*, which means "pure."

Guru Govind Singh chose the very first Khalsa in the town of Anandpur. The members were known as the *Panj Piare*, which means the "five loved ones." Guru Govind Singh knew that Sikhs needed to be spiritually stronger than their enemies if the Sikh faith and culture were going to survive.

> ### SPOTLIGHT
> #### "THE FIVE KS"
> These are the five special things that members of the Khalsa should wear.
> - *Kesh* uncut hair — a symbol of God's gifts
> - *Kangha* hair-comb — to show tidiness and discipline
> - *Kirpan* sword — a symbol of justice and spiritual power
> - *Kachh* short trousers — to show readiness for action
> - *Kara* steel wristlet — a symbol of unity and faith

The Guru gave the name *Singh*, meaning "lion," to the men in the Khalsa. He called the women *Kaur*, or "princess." These second names are still used by Sikhs today.

This engraving shows the first Khalsa members drinking amrit, offered by the Guru.

The ceremony for new Khalsa members is the same today as it was for the first group. It includes drinking *amrit*, the "water of life" or "holy nectar." This is made of sugar dissolved in water and stirred in a bowl with a short sword. It is a symbol of unity and equality.

THE LAST TASK

Guru Govind Singh knew that he was to be the last human Guru. It was now time to give over all power to God's teachings — the hymns of the Gurus. In 1706, Guru Govind Singh asked a Sikh scholar, Bhai Mani Singh, to add the hymns of Guru Tegh Bahadur to the Adi Granth. The Guru then gave the holy book a new name — the *Guru Granth Sahib*, which means "the volume which is the (Granth) most honored teacher." It is the guide and truth for all Sikhs, wherever they may be.

This is a new copy of the Guru Granth Sahib. The first copy is kept in a town called Kartarpur.

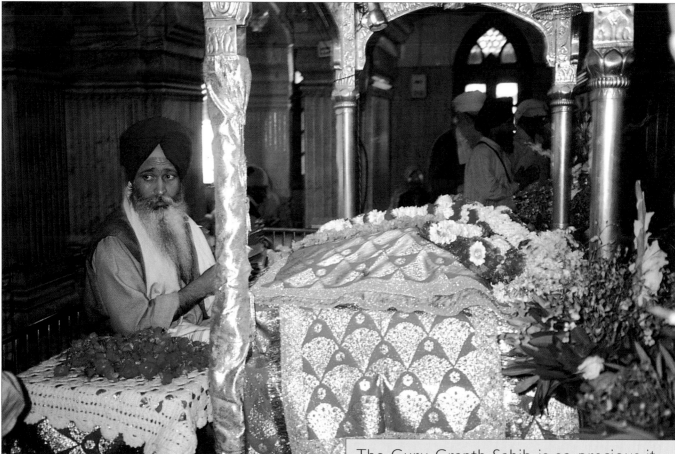

The Guru Granth Sahib is so precious it is wrapped in beautiful cloths and placed on a throne in many gurdwaras.

A BOOK FOR EVERYONE

The Guru Granth Sahib is the last Guru, and the most important of all for Sikhs, because it is the Word of God. Every day, Sikhs all over the world read their holy book or recite parts of it that they know by heart. It guides and helps them in all aspects of their lives.

When the Guru Granth Sahib was first put together, only a few copies were made — all by hand. The Sikh community did not need many copies because most Sikhs lived near one another in the Panjab. But as Sikhs began to move away, Sikh leaders realized that people might forget the teachings of the Guru Granth Sahib and be persuaded to join other religions. So, during the 19th century, hundreds of copies of the Guru Granth Sahib were printed.

Schools and Khalsa colleges were set up so that the Gurmukhi script (see page 8) and Sikh teachings could be studied. As a result, Sikh culture became stronger in India and people who moved to other countries had ways of teaching Sikh traditions to their children.

All the printed Gurmukhi copies of the Guru Granth Sahib that are used for worship have 1,430 pages. The hymns are laid out in exactly the same order. This means that Sikhs throughout the world can read and learn them in the same way. There are also translations of the Guru Granth Sahib in English, French, and other languages.

Students chat on their way to the Khalsa college in Amritsar, India.

INTERVIEW
I learn the Panjabi language and the writing because I want to find out about my religion – and because my parents want me to learn.
Navpreet, age 9, Coventry, England.

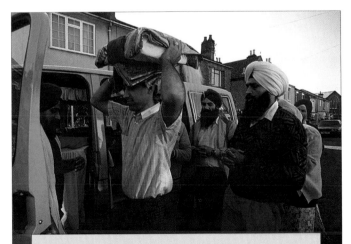
A copy of the Guru Granth Sahib is being carried from a gurdwara in England to a private house for a special ceremony.

LOOKING AFTER THE BOOK

It is very important to look after the Guru Granth Sahib properly and treat it with respect. Every day in the gurdwara, the holy book is taken from its nighttime resting place and put where all can see it in the main part of the temple, the Diwan hall.

The Guru Granth Sahib is wrapped in cloths called *rumalas*. Before it is read, the book is unwrapped and placed on a throne that is covered with a thick mattress and three cushions. Above the throne hangs a decorated canopy. A whisk, or *chauri*, is waved over the scriptures while they are being read.

Some people keep a copy of the Guru Granth Sahib at home. But to give it proper respect, it needs to be kept in a room of its own, which not all Sikhs can afford. So many families have a small book of readings to think about through the day. The book, called a *gutka*, is wrapped in a cloth and kept on a clean, high shelf.

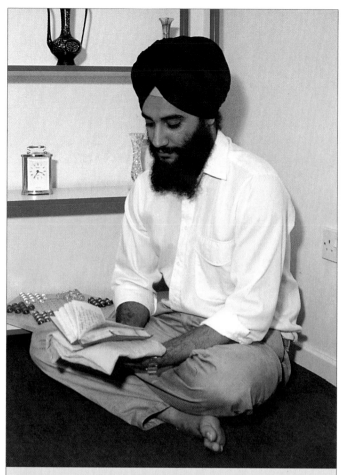

A copy of a *gutka*, is placed on a clean yellow cloth as it is being read.

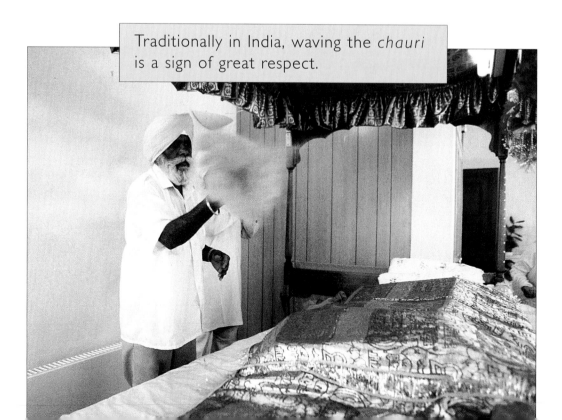

Traditionally in India, waving the *chauri* is a sign of great respect.

MAKING A CHAURI

YOU WILL NEED:

- *white or cream-colored wool*
- *a stick or long pencil*   • *scissors*
- *modeling clay*   • *aluminum foil*

WHAT TO DO:

1 Paint the stick or pencil with glue and cover with aluminum foil.

2 Mold the clay into bell shapes on the covered stick and cover the shapes with more foil.

3 Cut the wool into lengths of about 16 inches.

4 Tie the strands neatly to the end of the stick with another piece of wool.

GOING TO THE GURDWARA

PREPARING FOR THE GURDWARA

It is important for Sikhs to treat the gurdwara with honor, so before going there, everyone takes a bath. At the entrance to the Diwan hall, people remove their shoes and cover their heads. As people enter the main hall, they kneel in front of the Guru Granth Sahib and bow so that their foreheads touch the floor. After this, offerings are placed near the throne. These are often items of food which are later prepared as the langar (meal). Many people give money for charity.

When the offerings have been made, everyone sits cross-legged in front of the throne. Men and women sit in separate groups. There are no special places set aside for anyone, and there are no special priests, for everyone is meant to be treated as equal.

When Sikhs move from the Panjab, they often use existing buildings for their gurdwaras, as well as building new ones.

A DAY IN THE GURDWARA

The day begins very early in many gurdwaras, especially those in the Panjab. As early as four or five o'clock, a small group of Sikhs may carry the Guru Granth Sahib to its throne in the Diwan hall. The cloths around the holy book are changed for clean ones. Even at this hour of the morning, there is a small gathering of people. They sing hymns while this ceremony, called *Parkash*, takes place.

Next, the *Ardas* is spoken. This is a special prayer for guidance from

God, praising God's name. The Ardas is used on all important occasions. The Guru Granth Sahib is then opened at any page and the verse in the top left-hand corner is read aloud. This becomes the spiritual message for the day. It is called a *vak*.

The gathering then breaks up and people go about their daily work. Throughout the day, Sikhs come into the gurdwara. They receive guidance from the vak, which is written on a bulletin board. Some people arrange meetings in one of the small rooms in the gurdwara. Others eat in the langar room, joining anyone who is sitting there. The gurdwara is a place for meeting people as well as a place for worship.

Everyone sits down to listen and sing in the gurdwara. Children are not expected to be quiet!

The langar can be a very busy room. Huge cooking pots are needed to hold enough food for everyone.

In the evening, some Sikhs gather in the gurdwara for the last ceremony or the day. A song of praise, *Kirtan Sohila*, is read aloud and a prayer is spoken. The Guru Granth Sahib is closed and wrapped in a white cloth. One Sikh covers his or her head with a rumala and carries the holy book away on his or her head. A

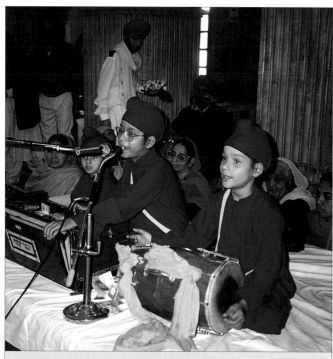

In Delhi, India, children are playing music inside the gurdwara, which can be used for various events.

Karah parsad is being given out at the Harimandir in Amritsar, India. The person receiving it always bows.

procession follows, led by someone slowly waving a chauri. Everyone chants a special hymn as the scriptures are taken to their resting place for the night.

For the family gathering at the gurdwara, Sikh communities use the official day of rest in the country in which they live. So in Canada, the United States, and Britain, for example, the family day at the gurdwara is on Sunday. On this day, people come to the gurdwara when they can and leave when they need to. But most try to stay until the Ardas is sung and the Guru Granth Sahib is opened to give the vak. Then everyone receives a small portion of sweet mixture that has been stirred in a bowl by a short sword (*kirpan*) during the Ardas. They eat this offering, called *karah parsad*, just as they are leaving the Diwan hall to go to the langar room.

MAKING KARAH PARSAD

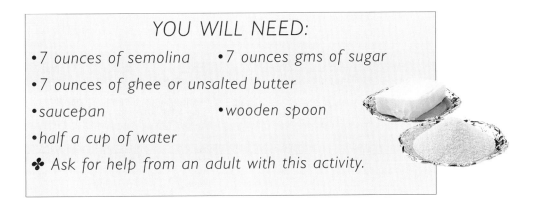

YOU WILL NEED:

- 7 ounces of semolina
- 7 ounces gms of sugar
- 7 ounces of ghee or unsalted butter
- saucepan
- wooden spoon
- half a cup of water
- ✿ Ask for help from an adult with this activity.

WHAT TO DO:

1 Wash your hands. Then melt the ghee or butter in a pan over a low heat.

3 Mix the sugar in well and add the water, watching out for steam. Cook slowly until the mixture thickens.

2 Add the semolina and cook it for 6 or 7 minutes until it is golden brown. Keep stirring so that it does not stick to the pan.

4 Serve the karah parsad in a shiny bowl and share it with your friends.

This is a turban shop, full of bright
lengths of cloth, in Amritsar, India.

BUSY LIVES

Sikhism is a way of life, not just a
way of worship. Sikh communities
have to survive and work in the
modern world just like every other.
But many Sikhs try to include prayer
and meditation in their everyday
lives, so that they will remember
God's name. For some, this means
spending some part of the day at the
gurdwara. For others, it could mean
meditating before breakfast and on
the way to work or school.

DRESSING DIFFERENTLY

It is often difficult to tell if someone
belongs to the Sikh community.
Many Sikhs have short, uncovered
hair and wear Western clothes,
particularly in the United States,
Canada, and Britain. But a lot of men
and boys show that they are Sikhs by
not cutting their hair, as Guru
Govind Singh requested. Young boys
have a small cloth to cover their hair
until they learn to tie a turban.
Some women and young girls dress

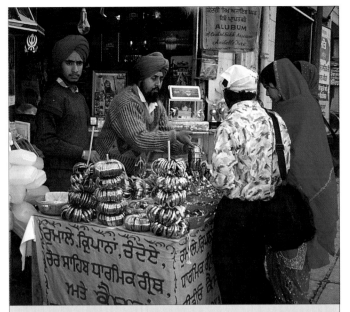

Steel bracelets are sold on a souvenir stall owned by Sikhs, near the Harimandir in Amritsar, India.

in long tunics and trousers, known as *salwar kamiz*. Their hair is uncut but usually tied back. Many Sikhs, both men and women, wear a *kara*, or steel bracelet. It reminds them of their faith throughout the day.

THE WORLD OF WORK

The Gurus stressed the importance of work to their followers. They especially encouraged people to set up their own businesses. In India, some traditional occupations for Sikhs were farming, building, and working as mechanics. But nowadays, Sikhs all over the world take up every kind of job or profession.

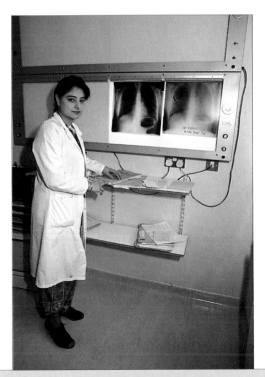

In England, a Sikh doctor examines X-rays. Sikh men and women enter all professions.

The traditional skills of carpenters are still highly valued. These Sikhs own a carpentry shop in Amritsar. India.

This cafe has bright pictures of the Gurus around the walls. You will see them in many Sikh shops, offices, and homes.

EATING AND DRINKING

Some Sikhs choose to be vegetarians. This is mainly because Sikhism began where there were large Hindu communities, and Hindus do not normally eat meat. The Gurus advised Sikhs to respect the rules of the people around them. The rules for eating are not very strict. But Guru Govind Singh gave very strong reasons why no one should drink alcohol, smoke tobacco, or take drugs. The Guru said that they are harmful to our bodies and our minds.

AFTER SCHOOL

Sikh children not only do their homework, play games, or watch television after school. Many also go to the gurdwara to practice singing hymns. Some learn to play musical instruments to accompany them. Outside India, the Panjabi language has to be taught at home and in the gurdwara. Learning the Gurmukhi script is difficult, but the original Guru Granth Sahib cannot be read without it.

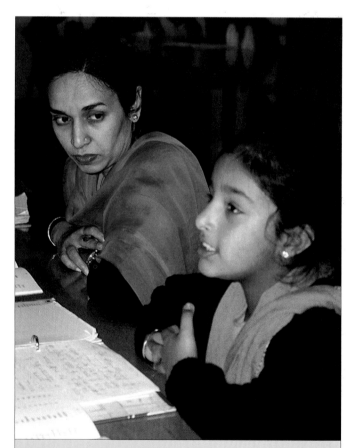

Outside India, some children go to the gurdwara after school for lessons to learn Panjabi and the Gurmukhi script.

Children often learn about their culture through listening to stories. The Gurus told their followers many stories. Some are really messages, explaining difficult ideas and decisions. Others are about the lives of the Gurus and the wonderful deeds they performed. These help to explain Sikh history.

The following story is good to think about as people go about their busy lives. It happened on Guru Nanak's long journey to the south.

At one place where he stopped, Guru Nanak was visited by a man called Duni Chand and his wife. Duni Chand was extremely rich. But like a lot of rich people, he occasionally wanted the approval of someone holy. So he came to pay his respects to Guru Nanak. Just as he was leaving, Guru Nanak pulled a needle from his bag and gave it to Duni Chand, saying, "Could you keep this safely for me? When I die, you can give it to me in the next world."

Duni Chand was a bit puzzled. "But how can anyone carry a needle into the next world?" he asked. "Then why have you collected all these riches if you can't take them with you?" replied the Guru. Duni Chand and his wife realized what Guru Nanak was trying to tell them. They went home and gave away all their wealth to the poor. And from then on, everything that they earned, they shared.

LET'S CELEBRATE!

FAMILY FESTIVALS

Sikhs share the special joys of family life with the whole community. Birth and marriage are welcomed with lively celebrations as well as gratitude to God.

Naming the baby in the gurdwara is one of the happiest and most important celebrations of all.

A NEW MEMBER

When a baby is born into a Sikh family, the baby's father tells the happy news to friends and relatives — he gives out boxes of candy, too! Presents of clothes and money are brought to the baby.

After two weeks, the baby is usually taken to the gurdwara on the day of the family gathering for the naming ceremony. The parents often bring new rumalas to cover the Guru Granth Sahib. After hymns of praise and thanks to God, the parents promise to bring up the new baby as a Sikh.

One person turns to the Guru Granth Sahib and sings the Ardas. The baby is laid in front of the scriptures while the granthi opens them to read the verse in the top left-hand corner. The first letter of the verse becomes the beginning letter of the baby's name. Now the parents can choose a name for their child, with much prompting from the rest of the people gathered there! The new name is followed with "Singh" if the child is a boy or "Kaur" if it is a girl (see page 14). When the granthi announces the name, everyone shouts the Sikh words of greeting, "Sat-Sri-Akal!" or "God is truth!"

GETTING MARRIED

The Gurus taught that family life is very important. So getting married is a serious business. Parents often help their children to choose a partner. The couple must be able to live together happily, so they discuss what they enjoy doing, the places they like visiting, and the things they believe in.

The bride's father has tied his daughter's scarf to the bridegroom's scarf, to show that she has left her own family.

In India and the Panjab, the wedding ceremony takes place in the gurdwara. In western nations, most couples get married at a registry office and have a wedding ceremony at the gurdwara, to comply with the country's laws The wedding hymn by Guru Ram Das is the central part of the ceremony. It is known as the Lavan. The couple walk clockwise around the Guru Granth Sahib as each of the four verses is sung.

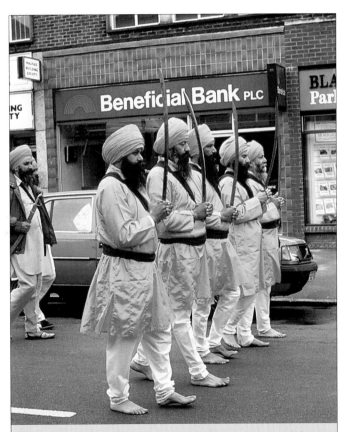

Five members of the Khalsa, dressed in the five "Ks," always lead processions held at gurpurbs.

ANNIVERSARIES

Festivals known as *gurpurbs* mark anniversaries. The births of Guru Nanak and Guru Govind Singh are honored in this way. In the gurdwaras, activities begin two days before the gurpurb with an *Akhand Path*. This continuous reading of the Guru Granth Sahib stops very early on the first morning of the gurpurb. Many people gather to hear the last verses of the scriptures. They also listen to readings and talks about the Guru who is being remembered.

Vaisakhi is also the day when Guru Govind Singh chose the members of the Khalsa. Here it is being celebrated with a fighting ritual.

SHARING FESTIVALS

Some Sikh festivals are held at the same time as Hindu celebratons. Sikhs and Hindus share some of the same ways of celebrating. But the Gurus gave each of these festivals a special meaning for their followers.

HAPPY NEW YEAR!

Sikhs celebrate New Year's Day, or *Vaisakhi*, on the same day as all Indians. Traditionally, it marks the end of the spring wheat harvest.

A FESTIVAL OF LIGHT

Diwali is probably the most spectacular of all celebrations for Sikhs and Hindus. It marks the end of the hot season and the start of winter, when crops can be sown. But Hindu religious stories also show that it is a time when good overcomes evil and light pushes away the darkness.

For Sikhs, Diwali marks the day when Guru Hargovind was released from prison. As the Guru made his way back to Amritsar, Sikh houses shone with candlelight in celebration of his return.

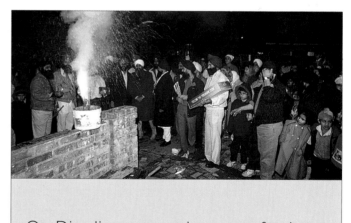

On Diwali, everyone has great fun in the streets as fireworks explode.

MAKING A SIKH FLAG

YOU WILL NEED

- *a stick or rod about 30 inches long*
- *a triangle of orange cloth, 14 inches on all sides*
- *a large square of orange cloth, 20 inches by 20 inches*
- *a square of blue cloth, 8 inches by 8 inches*
- *a square of paper, 8 inches by 8 inches*
- *a small piece of aluminum foil and cardboard*
- *glue and a brush, a pencil, and a pair of scissors*

The two edged sword (khanda), quoit (chakar), and sword (kirpan). These are symbols of unity, faith, and brotherhood.

WHAT TO DO:

1 On your square of paper, draw and cut out the symbols shown above right. Pin them on the blue cloth, and cut them out.

2 Glue the fabric symbols onto the orange triangle.

3 Fold the side of the yellow triangle around the stick or rod. Glue it down at the back. Make a khanda symbol from cardboard covered with foil. It should be 4 inches tall. Glue to the top of the stick.

The flag is respected as one of the symbols of the Sikh faith. So when you are not using it, cover it with the large piece of orange cloth.

31

GLOSSARY

Adi Granth "the first book" — "the most important book" for Sikhs; the first collection of the Gurus' hymns

Akhand Path a continuous reading of the Gurus' scriptures, used on special occasions

amrit "water of life" or "holy nectar"; a drink for members of the Khalsa

Ardas a prayer for guidance

bhagat bhani hymns written by some Hindus and Muslims

chauri a whisk waved in respect over the Guru Granth Sahib

Five "Ks" the five symbols worn by members of the Khalsa

granthi someone who takes care of the Book

gurdwara a Sikh temple

Gurmukhi the writing used in the scriptures

gurpurb a festival to mark an anniversary of the birth or death of a Guru

Guru one of the ten teachers and guides of Sikhs

Guru Granth Sahib the final collection of the Gurus' hymns

gutkha a small book of hymns and prayers

Harimandir the "Temple of God" in Amritsar

karah parsad a special, blessed, sweet given out in the gurdwara

Kaur "Princess" — a name given to Sikh girls

Khalsa the "pure ones" — forming a group of specially dedicated Sikhs

langar the dining room in the gurdwara, or the meal eaten there

Lavan a hymn sung at weddings

Mul Mantra the first verse written by the first Guru, Guru Nanak

Panjabi the language used in the Guru Granth Sahib and by many Sikhs — sometimes spelled "Punjabi"

rumalas cloths covering the Guru Granth Sahib

Singh "Lion" — a name given to Sikh boys

vak a daily spiritual message to help people through the day

INDEX